BUDDHIST
MEDITATIONS
for people on the go

BUDDHIST
MEDITATIONS
for people on the go

Gill Farrer-Halls

A GODSFIELD BOOK
www.godsfieldpress.com

First published in Great Britain in 2005
by Godsfield Press, a division of
Octopus Publishing Group Ltd
2-4 Heron Quays
Docklands
London E14 4JP

10 9 8 7 6 5 4 3 2 1

Printed and bound in China

ISBN 1 84181 243 9
EAN 9781841812434

CONTENTS

INTRODUCTION

Buddhist meditation is a practical way of avoiding dissatisfaction and finding true happiness. To achieve these goals, many Buddhist traditions teach a daily routine of sitting meditation aimed at developing insights that you can put into practice in daily life. All too often, however, meditators leave behind on the cushion the insights they gained during their sitting meditation. One meditator spent many long hours sitting in meditation, cultivating the mind of compassion towards 'all sentient [living] beings'. When he finally got up from his

cushion, he bumped into another meditator. 'Get out of my way', he shouted angrily. 'You're not all sentient beings!'

This book invites you to take into the everyday world the insights you have gained through sitting meditation. Each chapter introduces a traditional meditation topic, and provides step-by-step instructions for a guided 'on the cushion' meditation related to the topic. Then there is a unique list of 'on the go' suggestions, designed to help you gain a direct, experiential understanding of the teachings of the Buddha and put them into practice in your everyday life.

Follow the path

The order of chapters in this book loosely follows the traditional stages of the path known in Tibetan as *Lam Rim*, 'the graduated path towards enlightenment'. This sequence of meditation themes will take you from a consideration of the dissatisfactions inherent in your current situation right up to the joyful effort that will keep you on the path towards true happiness. Along the way, you will consider the importance of appreciating your life, gaining awareness of the consequences of your actions, practising generosity and patience, and recognizing the impermanence of everything – including your own life. Great Buddhist teachers of the past have carefully and insightfully put together this sequence of meditations as being ideally suited to further spiritual development.

Transform your everyday life

Though the meditation topics and sitting meditations presented here are traditional ones, often practised in the Tibetan Buddhist tradition, this book describes them in contemporary language, explaining all Buddhist terms clearly. If you spend time on these meditations, circling back over the sequence again and again, for a period of months or years, you will certainly gain insights that will help you become more compassionate towards yourself and others, and help you find more happiness in life.

Most of your life, however, is spent 'off the cushion' – in relationships with family and friends, working, shopping, eating out, and engaging in hobbies and other recreations. As you will discover when you try the 'on the go' suggestions, even the most materialistic aspects and activities of popular culture – movies and songs, a visit to the supermarket, an hour spent in a café – can be changed into an opportunity to experience first hand the transformative power of the Buddha's message. Practising meditation 'on the go' will help you realize that Buddhism is not simply a set of theoretical ideas, but rather a totally practical way of approaching the people and situations you encounter every day.

The practical spiritual method presented here encourages you to take responsibility for your own progress along the path to enlightenment. Living Buddhism 'on the go' supports and strengthens your meditative insights and helps you understand that the message of the Buddha is a complete way of being that can enlighten every aspect of your life.

Take responsibility

The common advice to meditators to seek out a properly qualified and experienced teacher for instruction and guidance is extremely good. Nonetheless, it is only through your own efforts and meditation practice that you will find genuine spiritual growth. The Buddha taught that the greatest teacher lies within your own consciousness, and that no one can do the hard work necessary for spiritual progress for you. In the end, we must each follow the path to enlightenment ourselves.

Basic mindfulness meditation

The second part of each chapter contains a traditional 'on the cushion' meditation related to the theme of the chapter. If you have never meditated before, here are some instructions for performing a basic meditation.

- *Find a quiet room where you will not be disturbed. Either cross your legs and sit on a cushion on the floor, or sit upright on a hard-backed chair; the important thing is to keep your back straight, and to be comfortable enough not to fidget.*

- *Shut, or half-shut, your eyes and place your hands in your lap. Bring your attention to your breathing, but don't try to change it. Simply observe the breath entering and leaving your body by focusing on the sensation at the tip of the nostrils, or on the rising and falling of your abdomen.*

- *When your mind wanders off into your usual thoughts and feelings, gently bring your attention back to the breath, without judgement.*

- *After 10–15 minutes, your mind may quieten; if it doesn't, it may be that you just never noticed all your thoughts before. Either way, you are now ready to practise the specific meditations described in each chapter of this book.*

I CAN'T GET NO SATISFACTION

Most people know the Rolling Stones song that this chapter borrows for its title. In the manner of all classic songs, the words resonate strongly – you yourself can't find lasting satisfaction. The song reminds you of this, but does not make you ask why it might be. You listen to the song, acknowledge the universal truth it points to, and carry on blindly looking for that elusive 'satisfaction'.

I once attended a Buddhist talk given by a wise Tibetan teacher who had recently heard the song '(I Can't Get No) Satisfaction' by a singer called 'Rolling Stone'. He clearly saw how most of us there had failed to find satisfaction from our worldly lifestyles. With obvious excitement he pointed out that, even in our materialistic culture, someone had had the insight that this did not bring satisfaction. With great compassion and humour, he told us that if 'Rolling Stone' stopped and meditated for a while he might find the satisfaction he so obviously wanted

Prince Siddhartha, who later became the Buddha when he attained enlightenment, also failed to find lasting satisfaction in his life of royal luxury. He was so moved by this dilemma that he resolved to keep on questioning why it might be until he found an answer. He ultimately realized that the two fundamental moments of life – birth and death – condition every moment in between. Yet people choose to live their lives as if they were immortal, as if death were a shadowy and distant future event. Denying death in this way cannot bring lasting satisfaction.

The Buddha's early life as Prince Siddhartha was filled with people dedicated to fulfilling his every wish. Yet he chose to renounce privilege, wealth and luxury, because they did not bring him enduring satisfaction. Of course he lived a pleasurable life

and he enjoyed this for a while, but eventually Siddhartha saw a sick person, an old person and a corpse. He then understood the illusory nature of wealth and luxury in the face of sickness, old age and death.

Siddhartha also saw a holy man living in poverty, but radiating deep inner peace. He thought that perhaps there was a way to find satisfaction beyond material wellbeing. He left the palace and joined the holy wandering men, learning meditation and practising asceticism. That feeling of satisfaction still eluded him. Realizing that neither material wellbeing nor ascetic mortification of the body brought satisfaction, Siddhartha sat under a tree and entered a deep meditation. After seven days he achieved enlightenment, an awakening to the truth of existence.

The four noble truths

Buddha's first teaching after enlightenment was about the 'four noble truths', addressing the thorny dilemma of why people don't find satisfaction in the things and activities they think will provide it.

First, Buddha pointed out that life is inherently unsatisfactory. The inescapable fact is that you will die. You also spend most of your time trying to satisfy your desires and avoid what you don't like. Yet you are continually faced with not getting what you want and having what you don't want. This is the nature of existence.

Secondly, Buddha looked at what causes this dissatisfaction. He realized that it is a person's own desires for some things, and aversions to others, that are the real cause of dissatisfaction. There is nothing

inherently satisfactory in the things you crave – the new car, bigger house or wonderful lover is not ultimately satisfying. Even if you get what you want, it changes, you become bored with it, or you want other things. This is the truth of impermanence – of both objects and your feelings for them. So the objects of your desire, whatever they might be, cannot bring you satisfaction, because your desires are what cause your dissatisfaction.

The third and fourth truths that Buddha taught bring better news. The third states that you can believe confidently that there is a way out of this circle of desire and dissatisfaction, because Buddha achieved enlightenment. This freedom from desire is called 'nirvana', the unconditioned state of liberation from dissatisfaction. Finally, the fourth noble truth is that there is a path you can follow that leads towards ending desire and the other causes of dissatisfaction. This path is based on love, wisdom, ethics, compassion and practising meditation.

On the cushion meditation:
DISSATISFACTION

The main point of this meditation is to become aware of just how much dissatisfaction exists in this world, both for you and for others. Traditionally, the subject of this meditation is 'suffering' rather than 'dissatisfaction', but in fact it includes all levels of unhappiness – from mild dissatisfaction through suffering to absolute anguish – and encompasses all states of being – physical, emotional and mental. What is the purpose of meditating on dissatisfaction, though? Surely you have enough dissatisfaction in your life without dwelling on it? Instead of increasing your dissatisfaction, however, this meditation will bring you a more realistic understanding of life.

The meditation has three parts. Begin with 10–15 minutes of basic mindfulness meditation (see page 9), and then spend 10 minutes meditating on each part.

Part 1: Suffering of suffering

The first aspect of dissatisfaction, or suffering, is the suffering of suffering. This includes all forms of easily noticed suffering, such as physical pain, mental turmoil and emotional distress.

• *Contemplate physical suffering, and remember times when you were in extreme pain. Then think about how many little aches and pains you experience throughout each day. This discomfort will only increase as you get older, so consider how unwise it is to be attached to your body.*

• *Contemplate emotional and mental suffering. Think of all the times when you have been lonely, depressed, jealous, anxious, angry and so on. There has hardly been a time when you felt no emotional or mental pain at all.*

• *Reflect that everyone – just like you – wants to be happy and avoid suffering. Dissatisfaction is universal, not personal.*

...everyone ... wants to be happy and avoid suffering.

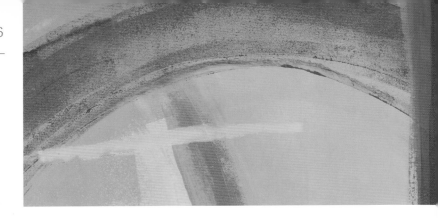

Part 2: Suffering of change

The second aspect is the suffering of change. This is a bit more subtle, as it concerns things you think will bring you happiness.

- *Contemplate all the wonderful experiences and objects you have had – special holidays, great sex, loving relationships, beautiful clothes, fast cars and so on. When they are over, you miss them, and this causes dissatisfaction.*

- *There is a saying, 'All good things come to an end' – reflect on this. Everything changes, and clinging to pleasure inevitably brings pain. Beauty fades, youth turns to old age and eventually death, money runs out, power and prestige finish. None of these things can bring lasting happiness.*

Part 3: All-pervasive suffering

The third aspect is all-pervasive suffering. This refers to the very nature of your existence, and how you foolishly believe you can find happiness in temporal, transient things while trying to forget the suffering of sickness and death.

- *Don't despair at this stage. Consider that there are ways to lessen suffering, and eventually remove the causes for dissatisfaction altogether, but it is important to acknowledge and understand the painful nature of existence first.*

- *Resolve to be less attached to things, and to accept that they will change. Think how everyone else is also caught up in dissatisfaction, and resolve to be kind to others as much as possible.*

- *Sit quietly for a few minutes before finishing your meditation.*

This meditation may have left you with unanswered questions, but the following chapters explore other ways to transform your dissatisfaction.

EXPERIENCE DISSATISFACTION on the go

Daily life provides many opportunities to feel dissatisfaction. You might experience discomfort and inconvenience while travelling to work, you might not be able to get what you want for lunch, or you might feel so tired in the evening that you fall asleep and miss seeing your friends. You might feel ill, lose your bag – the list is endless. Normally, you will try to fix the dissatisfaction as quickly as possible, but this never allows you to experience suffering and actually understand its nature.

Try the following exercises to help you experience dissatisfaction, but always keep a sense of humour. Life is full of little annoyances, and being able to see the funny side of them is a good antidote to misery or depression.

....

Investigate hunger

Next time you feel hungry and immediately think about getting something to eat, stop. This is an opportunity to appreciate the experience of hunger, to grasp what it really feels like. Usually, when

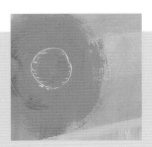

... life is inherently unsatisfactory ...

you feel hungry, all you can think about is eating to satisfy the craving; you rarely just allow the sensation to exist within you without doing something about it. Sit with your hunger and explore the feeling of dissatisfaction. After 10 minutes, you might notice that the feeling has either lessened or intensified; however it feels, you have really experienced hunger, not just tried to fix it as quickly as possible.

Relax pain

When you have a headache, bang your knee or experience some other hurt, use the opportunity to explore your pain. Imagine how you would cope if you were on a desert island and had no painkillers. Often, aversion to pain makes you fight against it, and wish it to go away quickly, but this can actually make the feeling worse. Sometimes, quietly relaxing into the sensation and mentally exploring it can lessen the pain. Even if pain levels remain the same or increase, you will have learnt something about the nature of pain by becoming familiar with the experience before you take painkillers to alleviate it.

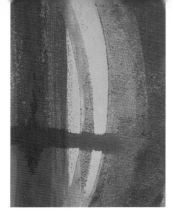

Notice dissatisfaction

Look around you at other people suffering; there are many opportunities. For example, in busy cities there are always people running for appointments, full of stress and anxiety about being late.

Stand quietly, or sit at a pavement café, and watch people pass by. Notice how many are obviously dissatisfied in some way. You might spot a beggar or a street person; see how most people try to avoid them. You might watch two people having an argument, which could cause a lot of suffering for them.

When you notice the suffering of others, it is much easier to feel compassion for them. You might feel the wish to help in some way, and if you can assist someone – without it becoming a problem for you – this is a good thing to do. Witnessing the everyday dissatisfactions of others also makes you realize that you all share these feelings, and that everyone seeks happiness and wants to avoid dissatisfaction.

Confront your usual reactions

Actively seek out a situation in which you normally feel uncomfortable – visit a busy shopping mall or a football game, or watch a movie with a subject you find distasteful. Don't just think how you dislike what's happening and wonder how you can escape it as quickly as possible. Instead, confront your usual reactions, to see if perhaps it might be your reaction to what you don't like that is causing the dissatisfaction rather than the situation itself. Look around you. Perhaps other people don't share your feelings of dissatisfaction, perhaps they are enjoying themselves – which means there is nothing in the situation itself that is causing dissatisfaction.

As long as you put yourself in a situation you normally dislike, it will give you the opportunity to discover something about your dissatisfaction. If you do learn something about your dissatisfaction, you might even be able to lessen it.

LUCKY TO BE ALIVE

Life is a wonderful gift but it is easy to take being alive for granted. You assume that you will wake up every morning, and that you will live to be old, although there is no certainty that such assumptions are correct. A Zen teacher once told his students, 'You are already dead, so the rest of your life is a bonus.' He meant that, because death is unavoidable, it helps to accept your death before it occurs so that you can make the most of life while you still have it.

So how do you make the most of your life? Contemporary society encourages people to acquire wealth and possessions in the mistaken belief that these things will bring happiness. Of course you need somewhere to live, food, clothes and other basics of existence, and you must work to provide these necessities for yourself, but unless your mind is content no amount of possessions can make you happy. Otherwise all rich people would be happy, which is clearly not the case.

Buddhism offers a different way to make the most of your life. Buddhist teachings refer to human existence as a precious human rebirth, because while you are alive you have the opportunity to develop your spiritual potential. The Buddhist view suggests that following the spiritual path, using your mind and heart to investigate what it means to be alive, leads towards finding true happiness. You can begin by appreciating your precious human life, your great good fortune at being alive and in a relatively pleasant situation. Most people don't live in extreme poverty, suffering from famine and disease, nor in the middle of a war zone. Yet television shows daily examples of the deprivations that some unfortunate people have to suffer. So reflect on your good fortune in having such a relatively comfortable life.

Train your mind

When your life is comfortable, with enough to eat, the benefit of education and many different opportunities, then you can make the most of your intelligent mind. This is not about how clever you are, but the acknowledgement of your wonderful mental ability, which is so much more sophisticated than that of other animals. The human brain is still many times faster and more complex than even the cleverest computer. Your greatest good fortune is your awareness, your moment-to-moment consciousness of yourself and your environment. When you train your mind through meditation, you can learn how to monitor and then choose your responses to what you encounter, and in this way be more skilful in your behaviour.

From negative to positive

Often you don't fully appreciate your life because you carry a negative self-image. Most people have a tendency to be impatient, or perhaps lazy or angry. Other people notice when you behave in a negative way, and are critical. Instead of accepting you have a fault and working towards transforming this negative emotion, you identify with it – 'I am an angry person, therefore I am bad'. Once you see yourself in

this negative light, it is very easy to become depressed and feel hopeless, unable to appreciate that you have good qualities too.

Meditation helps you to be realistic and accept yourself for who you are, with both good and bad traits. You can work towards transforming your negative emotions and strengthen the positive ones. In this way, you can really start to appreciate your precious human life, with the potential for spiritual development and, eventually, enlightenment.

The Vietnamese Buddhist teacher Thich Nhat Hanh gives many teachings on appreciating good fortune moment by moment. As you are a biological entity, your feelings and physical sensations are continually changing, and usually you don't realize how lucky you are not to be suffering. One of his teachings is 'the happiness of not having toothache', in which he encourages us to enjoy the pleasant sensation of not suffering that particular nasty pain. Because most people have had such pains, they know what it feels like and can appreciate the benefit of not having toothache.

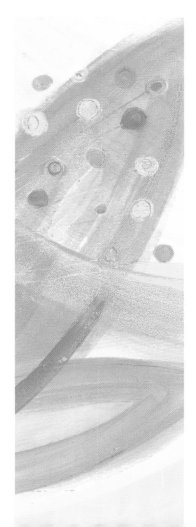

On the cushion meditation:
APPRECIATE YOUR LIFE

This meditation helps you to acknowledge the many good things you have in your life, and to realize your great good fortune at being born a human. Meditating on the inherent precious nature of human life is also a good way to dispel depression, feelings of worthlessness and hopelessness, and other negative emotions. The meditation encourages you to look at and clearly recognize all the good things you have in your human life, especially the rich opportunity to practise meditation and realize your spiritual potential. Animals don't have this precious opportunity; neither do humans who are trapped in war zones, mental dementia or extreme poverty. The meditation helps you to feel grateful and joyful about your good fortune, as well as compassion for other, less fortunate beings.

Begin the meditation session with 10–15 minutes of basic mindfulness meditation (see page 9), focusing on the breath.

- *Start by thinking about how you feel. Go beyond your usual quick, superficial responses and inquire deeply into your feelings about yourself. Most people have ambiguous feelings: they feel quite positive about some aspects of themselves, but they also hold negative feelings, such as habitual depression or feelings of inadequacy and hopelessness. Even if you feel positive and happy now, acknowledge to yourself that you do sometimes feel low, and determine to transform all your negative feelings.*

- *Think about what it would be like to be an animal, completely at the mercy of your desires, unable to exert control over your life. Animals have no opportunity for spiritual development. Reflect how fearful most wild animals and birds are of humans, and how they won't let humans come close to them. Imagine what it would be like to live in this constant state of fear and paranoia.*

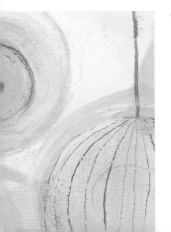

- *Now bring to mind how people living in extreme poverty might feel. Their lives are characterized by constant extreme hunger that they have no ability to relieve. They live in dreadful circumstances, with no easy access to clean water, shelter or medicines. Such people often have to beg, and suffer abuse from other people. Imagine how it would be to live like this.*

- *Imagine the life of someone living in a country where people are routinely tortured or killed for expressing their political or religious views. Think about how much fear and mental anguish such a person would feel all the time, not only afraid for their own personal safety but also knowing that their loved ones might be tortured or killed too.*

- *Now bring to mind your own problems and see how little they seem compared with those outlined above. Realize how insignificant in this broader context are such problems as a petty argument or missing an appointment. How lucky you are! Feel thankful for the opportunities and comforts you have in your life, and feel deep compassion for those less fortunate, whose lives are characterized by extreme suffering.*

- *Reflect upon your advantages, and try to appreciate your good fortune. You have friends and family who love and support you, and opportunities for education, travel, relationships and work. You have enough to eat, a roof over your head, access to doctors and medicines, and many other benefits. Most importantly, you have an intelligent*

You are already dead, so the rest of your life is a bonus.

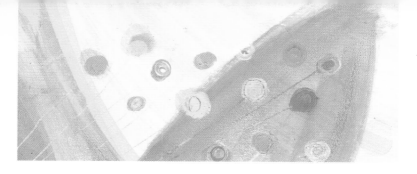

mind, and the opportunity to meditate, to investigate your mind and feelings, and the possibility to transform suffering and find happiness. What a rare and precious existence you enjoy compared to all those animals, birds, insects and less fortunate humans.

• *Contemplate how many things you could do with this precious life, but reflect how many of them bring only temporary satisfaction. Of course there is nothing wrong in having nice things and enjoying them, as long as you understand their limitations. Earning lots of money, indulging in sensual gratification and acquiring material possessions seem so limited when you have the ability to train your mind through meditation and the potential to attain enlightenment.*

• *Allow your mind to rest in simple appreciation and enjoyment of the many good things in your life. Feel happy for yourself, and compassion for those less fortunate.*

• *Finish your meditation with the wish that all beings might find happiness and avoid suffering.*

APPRECIATE YOUR LIFE
on the go

The following exercises take some of the
meditation subjects and expand them
into real life by creating opportunities to
witness the lives of other, less fortunate
beings. Also included are some quite
extreme exercises, which as well as being thrilling are designed to
startle habitual complacency about life. Be selective; if there is
something that you really don't want to do, then don't. Even doing just
one of these exercises is enough to bring the meditation alive.

Make contact with fear or poverty

Visit an asylum seekers' centre. You could ask to befriend someone
there and visit that person several times. Listen to their story and learn
about how it feels to have to have fled your own country. Alternatively,
visit a large city and go to one of the poorest districts. Observe the
standard of living there and take note of how it contrasts with the way
you live your own life.

Really try to get into the mind of someone living in poverty or
someone who has fled a totalitarian regime. Don't just read these words
and think how awful it would be; try to be in the minds of these people,
experiencing their fear and pain. This will help you appreciate your good
fortune in life in a very direct way.

Nature red in tooth and claw

Either watch a nature programme or go to a nature reserve or somewhere similar where there is a variety of wild animals. Observe closely how these animals are living, many of them in unpleasant circumstances. Look at a frog that has to live in a dirty pond, perhaps choked with weeds it has to fight its way through. The frog doesn't know where its next meal might come from, and lives in fear of being the heron's next meal. Nature programmes show graphic pictures of big animals eating little ones. As you watch the lion chasing its prey, remind yourself that the frightened antelope seeks only to find happiness and avoid suffering, just like you. Imagine what it would be like to be chased, caught and eaten alive.

The instinctive behaviour of animals

Watch a pet cat or dog. Observe the instinctive behaviour of the animal, how it seems to have little or no freedom to make the choices you take so readily for granted. Reflect how many more opportunities you have as a human to make conscious choices, and by choosing to behave ethically and compassionately you can transform your negative behaviour. A pet cat can never overcome its desire to kill small animals; its instinct is too strong. Yet, however strong your bad habits are, it is possible to overcome them through your strength of mind.

The thrill of being alive

Take a bungee jump, or try white-water rafting or any similarly exhilarating sport. As you go through the thrill and excitement of the activity, try to analyse what it is that is so exciting. One possibility is that you are playing with your own life; even though these sports are

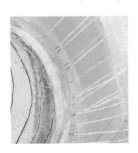

closely monitored and there are many safeguards in place, there is still an element of risk. The thrill you experience is actually the appreciation of being alive while doing something that is potentially life-threatening. Reflect upon what you feel before, during and after the event. This is a great way to be grateful for your precious life, while realizing that it could be over in a moment if something went wrong.

Earning lots of money ... [seems] so limited when you have the ability to train your mind through meditation and the potential to attain enlightenment.

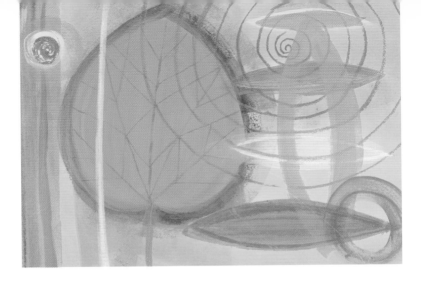

SHUFFLING OFF THIS MORTAL COIL

When thoughts of death arise, it seems scary, but you think of death as an event in the distant future and quickly put it out of your mind, or comfort yourself by thinking about dying peacefully when you are old. Only when someone you know dies, or gets a terminal illness, are you confronted with the stark reality of death. Witnessing the death of another person jolts you into accepting that you too will die.

It is certain you will die, but uncertain how or when this will happen. It is a foolish illusion to trust that you will live to be old; you have no guarantees on your life. Life is fragile, and depends on all the various parts and systems of your body working together satisfactorily, as well as continuously encountering conducive external environments. You depend on your breathing every moment of your life, but mostly you don't notice you are breathing. Yet if your breathing stopped for only a few minutes you would die.

This makes unpleasant reading at first, and you might think it a bit macabre or morbid to consider your own death. However, Buddha taught that – paradoxically – meditating on the certainty of death encourages you to live life more fully, enjoying each moment of your precious life as if it were the last. You tend to live your life planning for some mythical future, at the expense of living in the present moment. Although abandoning all considerations for the future would be foolish, nonetheless most people could live more in the present moment, enjoying their lives as they unfold.

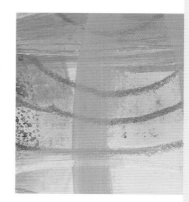

Meditating on death is a wonderful antidote to boredom and procrastination. Realizing the finite nature of your life is a wake-up call to help you make the most of it. This realization encourages you to do the things you believe will bring you happiness but that you tend to put off in the belief that you can do them later. My aged aunt told me shortly before she died that it was not the things she had done in her life that she had any regrets about, only the things she hadn't done.

Mental and spiritual preparation

Thinking about the inevitability of your own death might at first make you fall into a nihilistic depression. Conversely, you might think you should seek out hedonistic and materialistic pleasures to make the most of your life. Neither of these extremes is conducive to living life well and happily. You are more likely to find happiness in living life meaningfully, in harmony with others and doing things you feel are of

benefit, and that will bring pleasure to yourself and others. Learning about the Buddhist teachings and practising meditation are tried and trusted ways to find peace and happiness.

Everyone is equally powerless when death arrives; whether you are rich or poor, young or old, makes no difference. Acquiring lots of money and possessions is pointless as you cannot take them with you. All your wonderful experiences will be gone for ever, as will your loved ones, so although it is true that enjoying good times and relationships when they happen is sensible, spending all your life seeking them out is not. The only thing of any use when you die is a calm, tranquil mind, so that you can embrace death with peace and equanimity. The best time to start meditating and following the path to enlightenment is now, before this precious life is gone for ever.

In my teens, I had a friend called Madeleine. She was full of life and we had a lot of fun together. After college she went to live in rural France with her shepherd boyfriend. She embraced living close to nature and learnt how to practise local crafts to earn a living. She and her boyfriend had so many plans – they were going to travel the world and then settle down and have a family. Shortly after her twentieth birthday, she was killed in a car crash. It transpired that she and her boyfriend had been talking excitedly about their future plans and didn't notice a sharp bend in the road. I was very sad when I heard, but it made me realize that living in the present is more important than planning for a future that might never happen.

On the cushion meditation:
IMPERMANENCE

Meditating on the inevitability of death lessens fear about dying. Life is precious, but clinging to it is as unrealistic as trying to grasp hold of water. Confronting your death makes you investigate which of your activities are worthwhile and which are trivial, so that you can live life wisely, not wasting time on mundane pursuits. Becoming accustomed to the idea of your death means that when it arrives you can face it with a calm mind and die peacefully. Awareness of death in the midst of life keeps you focused on the present moment, so you live life fully.

Begin the meditation session with 10–15 minutes of basic mindfulness meditation (see page 9), focusing on the breath. The following meditation has three parts. Spend 10–15 minutes on each part, using meditation to go beyond intellectual concepts. Analyse each point, and investigate whether it is true. Make your meditation a deeply felt experience.

Part 1: The inevitability of death

- *Everyone dies sooner or later. Think of famous people in the past: kings, queens, writers, musicians and artists. They lived amazing lives and their achievements are noted in history books. Yet there is not a single person among them who didn't die. Now bring to mind people you once knew who have died. Nobody lives for ever.*

- *Science has made advances in curing disease, but there is no cure for death, even if life can be prolonged by a few years. Imagine all the billions of living beings alive now. There will be very few still alive in a hundred years' time. You will have died by then. Even now, your life span is decreasing moment by moment, so appreciate your life now. Realize that you have only a little time to meditate and calm your mind, since you still have to sleep, work, eat and so on, so determine to make the best use of your time.*

Part 2: The time and manner of death are uncertain

- *You have no way of knowing when – or how – you will die. Even young children die sometimes, so there is no guarantee of living the average life span. People die every day, but many did not expect to. Reflect on the different ways there are to die: car accidents, violence, illness, fire, drowning. Even life-affirming activities such as eating can kill you if you mistakenly eat poisonous food.*

- *Consider how fragile and vulnerable your body is. Even if you feel healthy now, this could change in a second. Recollect a time when you were really unwell, such as having flu or another debilitating illness. Recall a time when you hurt yourself, such as breaking a leg or arm, or cutting yourself on a knife. Remember how easily it happened, and how it could easily happen again. Reflect that if your injury had been more serious you could have died.*

Part 3: You can't take it with you

- *Only spiritual insight and a calm mind can help at death. The old saying 'You can't take it with you when you go' means your money and other possessions have no value for you once you are dead. Imagine you are lying on your deathbed. How does it feel? Nothing you turn to can help you. Think of all the effort you expended to acquire your possessions, and how they are now useless; your attachment to them only increases your suffering and prevents you dying peacefully.*

- *When you die, your loved ones surround you, but they can't help, however much they want to. They can't come with you, nor can they stop your death occurring, and you realize you will be separated from them forever. You will be separated from your body when you die, and even this most faithful companion during life is of no use at death. In fact, as your body weakens and degenerates, it causes only suffering.*

- *When you accept that your death is inevitable, meditating and developing spiritual insights help your mind become calm. Appreciate your life here and now. Breathe, and be aware of this ongoing connection with your life force. Don't feel depressed. There is nothing wrong with dying – it is a natural part of life. It is only your inability to accept your death that causes fear or depression. Meanwhile, you are alive right now and you have the opportunity to live life meaningfully, and practise meditation so that you can die peacefully.*

Everyone dies sooner or later.

EXPERIENCE IMPERMANENCE on the go

You know intellectually that everything – including yourself – is impermanent. Eventually you will die at an unspecified time in the future, even though you usually push aside thoughts of your own death. The meditation on death reinforces the reality of your death, and encourages you to make the most of life. These practical exercises take awareness of death into the present by encouraging you to witness the impermanence and passing away of other beings and objects.

Spend time among the dead

Visit a graveyard. Sit quietly for a while and feel the atmosphere. Notice if you can feel any association with death, such as a sense of peace, finality or quietness. Walk around and read the inscriptions on the gravestones. You will discover some people who lived to be old and others who died young. Sometimes a little extra information, beyond the dates of birth and death, is given about the deceased, such as the

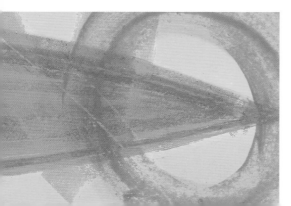

person being a dearly loved mother or brother. Think about your response to reading the inscriptions.

See how some graves are neglected; there may be no living relatives to care for and honour the grave, or they

may be too busy or have moved away. Perhaps the grave you are looking at is very old. Other graves may be quite new, and well tended, and have wreaths of flowers and plants. Reflect that death is a genuine reality for the grieving relatives who come to pay their respects to loved ones. Think how one day someone might be reading the inscription on your gravestone.

Photos last longer than people

Find a photo of someone you once knew but who has since died. If you don't have a photo of someone you knew personally, use a photo of a historical figure whom you have studied or admire. Look closely at the picture; notice the features on the face, and how their life experiences

might have shaped their expression. Reflect how this person was very much alive at one time, but now all that is left is an image. Imagine someone looking at a photo of you after you have died.

Rotting fruit

Select a piece of fruit and place it on a plate. Put the plate somewhere where you can observe it frequently. Make a point of examining it every day. Look for signs of change, discoloration, alterations in texture and smell. After a while, the fruit will show clear signs of rotting. Observe this process closely, and watch for any negative reactions you might feel. Examine any feelings of repulsion, or the wish to turn away. Develop an awareness that this process happens to all things that lived. Impermanence and death are characteristics of life.

The cycles of nature

Take a walk in a quiet, rural location. As you walk, observe closely what you see, and feel a part of the landscape you are walking through. Notice the characteristics of whichever season it is. If it is spring, new life is budding all around you, from what only a few months ago was a seemingly barren landscape. If it is autumn, some trees may appear to be dying, as they prepare for winter dormancy. Observe how beautiful their colours are. Your feelings may be tinged with sadness, since many things will die in this season. Reflect that the cycles of nature are based on impermanence, death and renewal, that this is simply the nature of being alive. Rejoice in your 'aliveness' now, because you realize this will not last for ever.

The only thing of any use when you die is a calm, tranquil mind ...

BEYOND DISCRIMINATION

Most of the time you are not aware of making judgements. Yet throughout a typical day you make many – some unconscious – about the people you meet, the experiences you have and the objects you see. For instance, you might like the person sitting opposite you on the train because she smiles, but dislike the waiter who serves you because he is sullen. You are constantly discriminating between what you like, dislike or feel indifferent towards.

This discriminating mind does not lead to happiness, because you encounter many more things and people you decide you don't like, or feel indifferent to, than those you decide you like. To move beyond discrimination you need to develop equanimity. Equanimity is a serene, even-minded state, unclouded by emotional agitation, that is the root of compassion towards all beings. When you investigate why you discriminate between people, categorizing them into friend, enemy and stranger, you see that your feelings about these different categories of people are based only on your self-centred concern. You like people who are kind to you, dislike those who hurt you and feel indifferent towards those you don't know. You judge everyone from this narrow perspective, rather than from an understanding of how you truly exist.

Equanimity requires both the determination to be even-minded at all times and insight into how people and things really exist, beyond your usual superficial understanding. When your mind is suffused with equanimity, you can accept difficulties and problems as easily as good fortune. This is because you see that all events are essentially neutral, that it is discrimination based on this 'I' and what it desires that causes you to judge things. You can try not to judge others, to treat everyone fairly and kindly, but until you see beyond the illusion of 'I' you run the risk of suppressing your feelings rather than transforming them.

If you investigate the 'I' that you each identify with, what do you find? There is only a sense of, a belief in, this 'I', there is nothing you can point to and say truly this is 'I'. If you point to the body, you find an organic, constantly changing entity; it has no permanence, so cannot be

the 'I'. The mind is also changing moment to moment; thoughts arise and pass. How can this changing mind be this strong sense of 'I'? If you look at other people, you see they also have this belief in their own illusory 'I'. Each person sees things from the perspective of the needs of this 'I'.

People actually exist interdependently, beyond the dictator 'I'. When you realize that all beings – not only 'I' – want to find happiness and avoid dissatisfaction, you can move beyond discrimination because you see that everyone has the same needs and desires as you. Other people don't just exist to satisfy your needs, nor do they exist according to how you judge them. For instance, there is nothing inherently bad about your enemies; these people have friends and families who love them.

Respect others

Respecting everyone's right to find happiness is a good start to practising equanimity. Reflect that your dear friend was once a stranger about whom you didn't care. You might fall out with this person tomorrow, but their wish to find happiness doesn't change, only your feelings towards them. Perhaps you don't like someone because of their appearance, but such superficial judgements are meaningless. If you catch yourself discriminating in this way, remind yourself how this person has as much right as you to be happy.

A Zen master had two disciples. The first meditated assiduously with a straight back and open eyes. The second always fell asleep during his meditation, his head falling forward onto his chest. One day the master told the second disciple to look at the first and take him as an example; his dedication was formidable and he rarely slept. Then the master told the first disciple to take the second as his example; his lack of attachment to formal meditation was so profound that whenever he meditated he entered such a deep concentration he was unaware of his body. The master was teaching the error of judging by appearances, and that discriminating in this way is foolish.

On the cushion meditation:
EQUANIMITY

This meditation involves thinking honestly about your relationships with other people. You will reflect on how your attitude towards others is usually based on what they can offer you, how they might be of benefit to you. This attitude is the root cause of discrimination. You like people who make you feel loved and secure, and you dislike people who hurt you. This way of thinking is based on the supremacy of what 'I' needs, above genuine consideration for others.

Begin the meditation session with 10–15 minutes of basic mindfulness meditation (see page 9), focusing on the breath. Then generate a strong motivation to engage in this meditation in order to develop equanimity.

- *Visualize three people standing in front of you. One person is your dear friend, for whom you feel much affection. The second is your enemy, someone you dislike strongly or who has hurt you in some way. The third is a stranger towards whom you feel indifferent. Spend a few minutes observing how your feelings differ towards these three people. Ask yourself why this might be.*

- *Now focus on your friend and your feelings towards this person. Notice how you feel warmth and affection towards your friend, safe in the conviction that this person is consistently kind to you. It is likely that you want your friend to be happy, and for the friendship to continue.*

- *Letting your feelings for your friend dissipate, bring your attention to your enemy. Observe your feelings towards this person, the sadness or anger you feel because they have hurt, annoyed or angered you. Perhaps you would be glad if they failed to find happiness, or suffered some misfortune. You might hope never to see them again.*

- *Letting your feelings for your enemy dissipate, bring to mind the stranger. What do you feel about this person? Your feelings towards the stranger are probably less intense than your affection for your friend and your dislike for your enemy. Perhaps you feel indifferent and don't really care whether or not this stranger finds happiness.*

- *Now try to recognize that how you feel about these three people is based solely on what they do for you at a given time. Imagine how you would feel if your friend suddenly turned against you. Your feelings of affection might turn to hostility. This change of heart shows you that your original feelings of affection were based on how this person could be of benefit to you rather than on any inherent qualities of the person.*

- *Think of your enemy and how a change of circumstances might transform your feelings for them. What might happen if they offered you some kindness or assistance? Perhaps you would feel that you had misjudged them and decide that they are not so bad after all. In fact, if the person was repeatedly kind to you, your resentment might turn to affection.*

- *The same is true about your indifference towards the stranger. Imagine that you meet, have a conversation and realize you have a lot in common. Soon feelings of friendship might arise.*

- *Reflect on the fragility of all human relationships, how impermanent they are and how easily they can change. There is no logical reason why you should have feelings of affection, dislike and indifference* towards other people. Your friend was a stranger before you met, your enemy might have been a former friend with whom you fell out and the stranger could easily become a friend or an enemy.

- Realize that the only lasting thing you have in common is that you all wish to be happy and not to suffer. This common goal shared by all beings is a sound basis for developing equanimity – the even-mindedness that is the root of compassion for all. Understand the foolishness of discriminating between people based on a self-centred viewpoint and reflect that everyone deserves kindness and compassion.

- Conclude the meditation by resolving to have respect, concern and regard for everyone, whatever your relationship, because you understand that discrimination based on personal preference is purely arbitrary. Relationships change, and developing equanimity and compassion for all is a wise response to this impermanent world.

Other people don't exist to satisfy your needs ...

PRACTISE EQUANIMITY on the go

This exercise will deepen your understanding of how you instinctively make judgements about people. After practising the exercise a few times, you may realize the foolishness of discriminating on such an arbitrary basis as personal like and dislike. This will help you develop a real sense of compassion towards others, regardless of your initial judgements about them.

Watch the world go by

You will need a whole morning or afternoon to do this exercise properly; there is no sense in rushing it, or feeling pressured because you need to go and do something else. In this relaxed frame of mind, choose a café that has seats on the street, or find a window seat with a good view of passers-by. Get yourself a drink and sit comfortably, watching the world go by.

Look at how each person walks. Some people will be rushing, glancing at their watch. Others, perhaps tourists, will be dawdling, looking around and noticing the scenery. Some people are dressed smartly; others are a bit scruffy. Some people look as if they are familiar with the location; others might look foreign, or behave as if they don't know the place.

Now examine your feelings about each person. See if you can catch yourself making judgements such as 'This man is really scruffy – I don't like people who neglect their appearance', 'I fancy him!' or 'Look at that woman dawdling, she's just another wretched tourist'. Contained within these judgements are the seeds of discrimination. Now contemplate that each person who passes by has goals essentially the same as yours; everyone wants to be happy. Consider that each person wants to find happiness each in their own way, and respect this.

Next time someone you don't like the look of passes by, try to feel compassion for them. This person is simply living their life, with dreams and aspirations just like you. If you met this person after having let go of your discrimination against him or her, you might be surprised to find that you actually liked the person. Reflecting on your judgements in this way will help stop them arising, and allow compassion to manifest itself in your consciousness instead.

RIPPLES IN THE POND

Most people have heard of 'karma', meaning fate or fortune. Although not incorrect, this interpretation misses the subtle meaning and complexities of karma. Karma means actions that are willed or meant, that have intention behind them. However, even if you do something instinctively without thinking, there is still some unconscious intention. So all your thoughts and actions create karma, and – like ripples in the pond – the effects of these are fast-growing and inevitable.

Mental karma is created by the mind and thoughts, verbal karma by speech, and bodily karma by physical actions. Mental karma is the most significant because, although it exists on its own, it is also the origin of the other two types of karma. In other words, you always think before you speak or physically do something – however briefly – and these thoughts influence what you say and do.

Actions that are skilful, beneficial and good create positive karma; actions that are unskilful, harmful and bad create negative karma. Therefore, negative karma arises from actions that are driven by ignorance, hostility and greed, such as killing, stealing and lying. Positive karma arises from actions driven by wisdom, love and renunciation, such as acting selflessly with kindness, love and compassion.

Three stages must occur for an action to be complete: motivation to perform the action, successful fulfilment of the action and satisfaction on completing the action. If only one or two stages are fulfilled, the karma created is less, while a fully completed action generates greater karmic consequences. For example, if you mistakenly squash an insect and are sorry that you killed it, only the action itself has occurred; there was no intention or satisfaction. The karmic consequences are therefore considerably less than if you deliberately jumped on the insect and were happy that you had successfully killed it.

Cause and effect

Karma is called the 'law of cause and effect'. This means that every action, however tiny or seemingly insignificant, creates a cause for an eventual result. Mostly, however, your actions are influenced by many factors throughout your life – and different lifetimes – that intermingle. So you often cannot clearly see how karma operates. Many of your actions create karmic consequences that are not experienced immediately. So, for example, when you see a kind, generous, honest person suffering, you can rest assured he or she will eventually experience positive consequences of their good actions, although this may be in a later life.

Certain behaviour creates specific karmic consequences. For instance, a person who easily finds wealth and prosperity in this life created the cause by being generous in a previous existence. Beauty is the result of pure ethical behaviour in a past life, while people who find it difficult to express themselves, or are not believed or taken seriously,

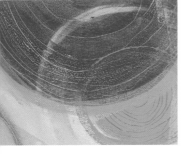

created the cause by lying in a previous existence. You can see from these examples that karma is interlinked with ethical, responsible behaviour – in other words, you reap what you sow.

Rebirth is a difficult concept, but looking at talent helps to understand karma going from one life to the next. People with outstanding musical talent often describe their ability as if they already knew how to play music when they first started.

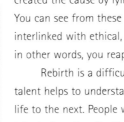

Both Mozart and Jimmy Hendrix, for example, learnt music quickly from an early age, and had an inner sense of harmony and rhythm. It seems that musical training in a previous life created karma for the musical ability to be carried over to a new life. Behavioural patterns are also influenced by karma. For instance, if someone tends to get angry easily this is a karmic consequence of previous angry behaviour.

Karma makes one thing very clear: you are responsible for whatever occurs in your lives. The person who has happiness, health and success created the causes for a pleasant life by performing positive actions in previous lives. Those who suffer illness and poverty likewise created the causes for their unpleasant experiences by committing negative actions. Most people have a mixture of good and bad experiences throughout their lives, reflecting their different karma. So karma is not fatalistic. Consciously trying to act with wisdom, kindness and compassion creates positive karma.

Black and white stones

A Buddhist monk practised meditation in front of two piles of stones – one of black stones and the other of white. As each thought arose in his mind, he analysed whether it was good or bad. For every good thought, he took a white stone and placed it on his right side; for every bad thought, he took a black stone and placed it on his left. Each night he checked the day's stones and renewed his resolve to eliminate the black stones altogether.

On the cushion meditation:
KARMA

You have just read that karma is intentional action, that past actions determine your experiences now, and that your current actions condition the quality of life to come. However, karma functions in an extremely complex way, and is difficult to witness in action. Meditating on the mind affords an opportunity to witness the arising and passing of thoughts and feelings. Because these are conditioned by your habitual instincts and tendencies, observing them gives a glimpse into how karma operates in the mind.

Begin the meditation session with 10–15 minutes of basic mindfulness meditation (see page 9), focusing on the breath. Observe how one exhalation causes and conditions the next inhalation. For instance, if you take a particularly deep breath in, the out breath will be affected, and will be equally deep. Even with breathing normally, each inhalation causes an exhalation, and without this basic bodily function you would cease to exist.

- *Reflect that your personality and experiences in this life are conditioned by the karma from previous existences. Although at death your personality – the 'I' sense you feel – dies, nonetheless the karma it created will go on to shape the personality of the next life.*

- *Look at one of your habitual tendencies, such as getting angry quickly. Investigate why you might feel like this so often. Because your mind is familiar with feelings of anger from previous occasions, perhaps it is easy for the mind to feel angry. The anger is self-perpetuating, and not only causes you suffering now, but creates the karma for you to feel anger again*

*soon. Determine to break this karmic cycle of anger, and promise
yourself that, next time you feel anger starting, you will stop. Reflect
how anger is negative and causes only suffering to you and to those
around you. Breathe deeply and let the anger go. After some time of
not indulging your anger, you will notice that you don't tend to feel
angry so often or so quickly.*

- *Now observe your current state of mind. What thoughts and feelings
  are flickering through it? Observe them arising and passing; don't judge
  them in any way. Think of the mind itself as being like a river, flowing
  along continuously with, deep beneath the surface, thoughts and
  feelings arising and passing. Try to sense the continuity of your mind,
  this flowing stream of consciousness, beyond its transitory contents.*

- *Bring your attention to the arising of thoughts. When you observe a
  thought or feeling arise, try to ascertain if it was caused from previous
  thoughts, and note how it might act as a cause for future thoughts. For
  instance, thinking 'It's a nice sunny day today' might lead to thinking*

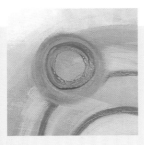

*... karma functions in an
extremely complex way ...*

about memories of previous
sunny days or to fantasies
of a future holiday. If an
intuition arises about how
your thoughts condition one
another in this manner, stay
with it for as long as it lasts.

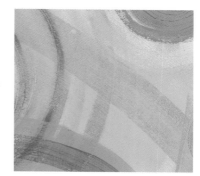

- Now start to trace your past
mental experiences, starting
with earlier today and going back days, weeks and years. Don't allow
yourself to get caught in reminiscences; the point of the meditation is
to try to understand how thoughts and feelings have a cause and an
effect. For instance, recollecting an old sad, painful memory might
make you feel sad and hurt now in the present, even though there is
nothing in the present moment to cause you to feel sad.

- Ask yourself if these old thoughts are part of who you are now. Did they
condition who you have become now?

- Return to watching the breath, and the arising and passing of
thoughts. Try to keep a sense of the underlying continuity of the mind
as you move from your meditation into your everyday life.

EXPERIENCE KARMA on the go

The traditional Buddhist story about the black and white stones (see
page 59) is an inspiration to try out the following practical exercises,
which are designed to help you become aware of the effects of your
everyday thoughts and actions. Although the monk's practice might be
a little impractical for those living in the modern world, nonetheless
you could spend a little time each night recalling your thoughts and
actions. Look at the number of your positive and negative thoughts and
actions during the day, as an encouragement to focus on developing
skilful behaviour.

....

Smile

As you go about your daily life, you are usually so preoccupied with thoughts of what you have to do, and feelings of stress and pressure, that you often don't notice or take into account the various people you encounter. Smiling at others is a simple yet effective way of acknowledging each other that many people respond to immediately and positively. A smile is an outward sign of wishing others wellbeing and happiness, and – if the smile is heartfelt and genuine – might cause them to respond in kind.

There are situations where this exercise might not be appropriate, as you do not want to generate unwanted attention from needy or troubled people. So choose situations in which you feel comfortable and safe, and smile at other people – you may be surprised how many people smile back at you, and how it creates a good, positive, happy feeling for all concerned.

A kind word

You can develop the smiling exercise a little further in some situations. Consider the people who serve you in shops, restaurants, ticket offices and so on. I have practical experience of this kind of serving work. It is a little shocking when you realize that most people are too busy or preoccupied to even acknowledge you as a person; you are simply a functionary who is going to provide them with an item, and you had better be quick and efficient about it. This can be demoralizing for the server, causing them to become sullen and resentful. This attitude is then transmitted to the next customer and a negative, unhappy feeling can prevail.

Try noticing and acknowledging the next person who serves you. Make eye contact, smile and say something kind. Even if the server does not respond, it doesn't matter. Karma is not always instant, but the server may well feel a little happier, even if he or she doesn't show it. The point of the exercise is to be kind without expectation, to create a little positive karma and spread happiness in daily life.

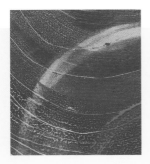

Actions that are skilful, beneficial and good create positive karma ...

You might observe the opposite: a customer being rude and surly to a server, or the other way round. Feel how negative the whole atmosphere becomes, and how other people bow their heads, feeling bad and not wanting to be involved. Avoiding rudeness – even if you don't feel like being kind all the time – at least prevents causing negative karma.

THE OPEN HEART

Loving kindness is a powerful Buddhist practice that develops spaciousness of mind and openness of heart. To practise, you need to cultivate benevolent feelings and empathy towards others, and to try to understand their feelings and needs, so you can respond with kindness in appropriate ways. Buddhist teachers say that, even if you find it hard to understand or practise the other Buddhist teachings, the least you can do is be kind, compassionate and loving towards others.

To practise loving kindness towards others, you need first to be able to be kind and loving towards yourself. If you cannot wish yourself happiness and wellbeing, how can you authentically wish others well? Although you are preoccupied with looking after your material wellbeing, it is nonetheless easy to feel undeserving of receiving love and happiness; a sense of inadequacy can also prevent you feeling loved. Loving kindness starts in your own heart, and then spreads outwards to all beings, so a sense of self-worth naturally transforms into concern for others.

Loving kindness is as much a state of mind, or an attitude, as any actual act of kindness. For example, if you are helpful to a work colleague, but do so with a hard heart and through gritted teeth because you don't like him or her, this is not authentic loving kindness. You are being 'kind' because you feel you ought to, not because of any real concern for the other person. So be realistic about your ability. Learning when you can act with authentic loving kindness and when you are simply unable to is important. You might have the intention to

be kind but not succeed, and then feel disappointed and angry when you fail.

You can't expect to like everyone you encounter, and some people are harder than others to be around. It is easy to be kind to people you instinctively like, those who are agreeable to you, but much harder to be kind to those who upset you through their unkind behaviour. You can at least refrain from being unkind to those you don't like. Reflect that this unpleasant person must be suffering to behave in such a nasty way, and therefore is in need of loving kindness. If you try hard to show loving kindness to that unkind person, it might help them change their negative behaviour.

Sometimes you don't feel as if you have much kindness to offer others, especially when you are suffering in some way. Yet even when you feel bad you can still be polite and courteous to other people, remembering to say thank you and so on. These little acts of kindness can actually help you feel better, since people often respond immediately with kindness in return. This creates a sense of kinship with others, and means you don't feel so alone, which will often improve your mood.

Loving kindness in practice

The more you practise loving kindness instead of selfishness, the more you will become accustomed to behaving in a kind, loving manner. When you practise loving kindness to others as often as you can over a long time, it becomes an automatic reaction, without thought. You simply reach out to help others as if it were you who was suffering. Then eventually your feelings of loving kindness become spontaneous, and you no longer think you must act kindly. You simply feel loving kindness towards others from the bottom of your heart.

Acts of loving kindness need not be grand or dramatic. Many acts of loving kindness take only a few seconds, such as helping a mother carry her pushchair up some stairs or opening a door for someone who has their hands full, but experiencing a kind act like this can make someone happy all day. Loving kindness also does not require great wealth. Even if you are materially poor, you can still offer others loving kindness.

A Buddhist hermit was meditating in his cave one night when he heard a group of thieves sneaking in. The hermit knew he had few possessions and they would not find much, so he got up and went over to them. They stood there in surprise as he offered them his few possessions, and suggested they could also take the little food he had in case they were hungry. The thieves felt so ashamed of their attempted theft in the face of such loving kindness that they fell down in front of the hermit and begged his forgiveness.

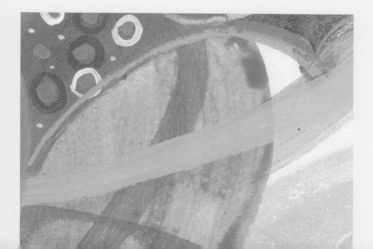

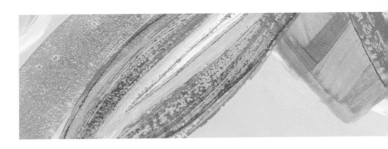

On the cushion meditation:
LOVING KINDNESS

Loving kindness meditation puts you in contact with your natural ability to love others, and to wish them wellbeing and happiness. This feeling is cultivated with concentration and sincerity, and then directed systematically towards yourself, friends, strangers, enemies and eventually to all beings everywhere.

This expansion of loving kindness from yourself to others in ever-widening circles generates feelings of harmony and peace. With practice, eventually you can genuinely feel loving kindness towards all beings, regardless of their relationship to you.

Begin the meditation session with 10–15 minutes of basic mindfulness meditation (see page 9), focusing on the breath. As well as watching the breath, try to discover within your heart a warm, caring feeling towards all life.

- *Start to develop loving kindness towards yourself. Accept yourself as a human being, as someone with both faults and good qualities, but someone who has the right to try to find happiness and avoid suffering. Perhaps sometimes you feel you don't deserve to be happy, or you judge yourself unkindly. Soften these harsh feelings and be kind to yourself, feeling compassion for this suffering being. Remind yourself that developing loving kindness towards yourself is the first step towards developing loving kindness towards others.*

- *Silently say to yourself, 'May I live in safety. May I experience mental happiness, peace and joy, physical happiness and health. May my daily life go easily, without difficulties.' Repeat these phrases silently several times, at the same time reflecting on the meaning behind the words. These are traditional phrases, but you can amend them if you wish to make them more meaningful for you. Try to allow the phrases to emerge naturally from your heart; it is important to cultivate your feelings rather than your intellect.*

- *After a few minutes, bring to mind someone who has helped you in some way. This person might be a benefactor, teacher, parent, spouse or lover. It is important to choose someone for whom you feel great respect, love and gratitude. Repeat the phrases above, using that person's name. Remember their great kindness towards you, and feel loving kindness towards them.*

- *After a few minutes, include a good friend, someone for whom you feel real affection, and repeat the phrases using their name.*

- *Now include someone towards whom you have no strong feelings either way. This is a bit more difficult, so remind yourself that this person you feel neutral towards has as much right as everyone else to find freedom from suffering and to achieve happiness. There is no reason not to wish this person loving kindness, and there is no danger that your loving kindness will run out; you have a bottomless well of loving kindness in your heart. Generate a feeling of loving kindness in your heart towards this person.*

- *Now include an enemy, someone who has harmed you or towards whom you have strong negative feelings. This can be really difficult, so allow yourself as much time as you need. Reflect that you don't have to like the person, or condone their negative behaviour, but you can develop loving kindness towards them, and not wish them harm. Often people who behave badly experience much suffering, so offering them* genuine loving kindness might help them feel and behave with more consideration. Remember that such people are not their bad actions; they are complex beings with many possibly conflicting feelings and difficult circumstances affecting how they behave. Recall that sometimes you too behave badly towards others, but that you would like those people to forgive you and not wish you harm. Try hard to generate loving kindness towards this person.

• Finally include all beings everywhere, and radiate feelings of loving kindness towards them all. Reflect that we are all interdependent, no one is an isolated being, and we all affect each other. If you like, you can visualize sending streams of loving kindness from your heart as white or gold light radiating out to fill the whole world. Rest in the warm feeling of all-pervasive loving kindness for as long as you wish. Dedicate the merit from this meditation on loving kindness to the happiness of all beings everywhere.

Many acts of loving kindness take only a few seconds ...

PRACTISE LOVING KINDNESS on the go

Taking the meditation on loving kindness off the cushion into daily life will help you feel less self-centred and self-concerned. Actively finding ways to help others, focusing on their wellbeing rather than your own, will make you feel happy, content and worthwhile. Paradoxically, letting go of your self-concern and practising acts of loving kindness towards others will lift your own spirits much more than when you try selfishly to find happiness, ignoring the wellbeing of those around you.

Last seat on the bus

Imagine it is late afternoon; everywhere people are leaving work, and everyone is tired after a long day at the office. People queue for ages for the bus or train; it arrives and there is a mad scramble to get on and grab a seat. You find yourself next to another person and you have

a split second either to dive into the last empty seat or to offer it to the other person. What do you do?

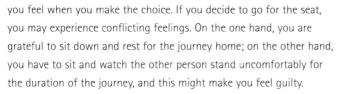

You have two options in this scenario: to give up the seat or to take it. You have probably been in this situation many times, but next time it happens observe closely how you feel when you make the choice. If you decide to go for the seat, you may experience conflicting feelings. On the one hand, you are grateful to sit down and rest for the journey home; on the other hand, you have to sit and watch the other person stand uncomfortably for the duration of the journey, and this might make you feel guilty.

Alternatively, if you give up the seat, you see how grateful the person is. So, although you may have to stand uncomfortably, you feel good inside. You have, in this small but significant way, contributed to someone's wellbeing, with a practical expression of loving kindness. The person may smile or offer you thanks, but even if the person doesn't, you know he or she feels happy being able to sit down.

Remember to be realistic; each time you have the choice, assess how you feel. If you have had a particularly hard day, you may feel resentful if you give up chasing the empty seat. This is then not a skilful act of loving kindness. However, you can try more often to let someone else have the seat. Reflect that you have made the other person feel happy, and that you also feel glad to have offered the person a little act of loving kindness.

Take time for tourists

If you live in an attractive place or a large city, you may often encounter tourists or strangers. These people seem to wander around aimlessly, and it can be irritating if they get in your way as you go about your daily life. Sometimes tourists get lost and need to ask someone local to help them find their way. It is tempting to rush past and not take the time to help them, or to answer briefly and rush off.

Imagine if you were lost how grateful you would be for assistance that was given with kindness. A few minutes will often not make much difference to your daily schedule, but the assistance you offer can be really helpful to a lost tourist. Next time someone stops you and asks for directions, observe your feelings. If you feel irritated, put yourself in this person's place. It takes only a few minutes to smile, be courteous, and answer the question as best you can. This example of practical loving kindness can make a strong impression on the lost person, and help him or her feel they are among friends, and less vulnerable.

....

A helping hand

When you see a mother struggling with a young child and pushchair, why not stop and offer to help her? Perhaps you feel afraid that she might resent your offer of help, that she thinks you feel she can't cope, but this is not a valid reason not to offer assistance. If she doesn't want help, she will tell you, but if you don't offer then you will have lost an opportunity to give someone a simple but effective act of loving kindness. Start looking for similar opportunities to help others. For example, someone with his hands full might appreciate it if you hold the door open for him. When you offer practical loving kindness like this, you will find not only that the people you help feel grateful but that you feel happy and worthwhile too.

Loving kindness starts in your own heart ...

GIVING IS ITS
OWN REWARD

When people think of giving, they normally think of giving material gifts. However, the traditional Buddhist teachings on generosity include giving protection and refuge to those in fear or danger, and giving genuine information about Buddhism, if one is requested to do so. The latter three categories of giving reveal a deeper meaning – that giving involves something of yourself, not just material objects.

Embracing the idea of giving to others your time, energy, attention and knowledge, as well as material things, will help you realize that giving includes cultivating a generous frame of mind as well as practising actual acts of generosity. More specifically, the essence of giving combines the spirit of generosity with actual acts of giving. When you give something to someone purely, with no expectation of gratitude or a return gift, then your sincerity shines through your act of giving, and the person receiving the gift also receives the mind and spirit of generosity.

Giving is not dependent on wealth, and even if you are materially poor there are still many things you can give. Time is often a precious commodity in the contemporary world, and giving someone the gift of your time, perhaps just through listening, can be an act of real generosity. In the same way, a material gift given resentfully or carelessly is not pure generosity. If you do not give your full attention to others when listening to them, this is also not giving purely. The generosity is less if the spirit of giving is absent from the act.

You must give from your heart as well as your pocket for the act of giving material objects to be real. Giving someone an expensive gift with a mean attitude and a closed mind is not being generous. Giving a gift because it is expected of you – and this is the spirit in which you approach choosing, buying and giving the gift – is not real generosity. A small, inexpensive gift given purely with love creates more happiness for the giver and receiver than an expensive gift given resentfully or with the expectation of receiving something in return.

Be realistic about how much you can afford to give, both of material gifts and of your time and energy. Giving so much that you impoverish yourself unnecessarily is unskilful giving. However, you can often give a little more than you think you can. Give material benefit and attention to others as often as you can afford to, because generosity is a powerful antidote to attachment and greed. By taking every opportunity that arises to practise generosity, gradually you will begin to develop an authentic giving mind, and transform attachment into generosity.

Giving helpful advice sincerely is generosity, as is giving knowledge and information. These acts of giving can be of much benefit to others, but be careful only to give these when asked. Otherwise you may find you are also trying to demonstrate how clever

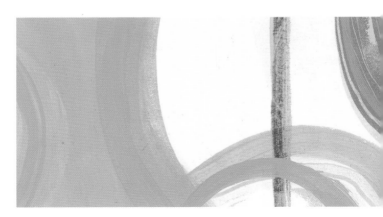

you are. Remember that not all acts of generosity are skilful. An example of unskilful giving is when someone gives damaging substances, such as tobacco, to another person, thereby contributing to their ill health by encouraging them to smoke.

Receive with grace

Receiving is an integral part of giving, and you can try to be skilful in how you receive the gifts of others. Even if you are given something you neither want nor like, try to be gracious in the receiving of it, and thank the person wholeheartedly. By accepting the gift courteously and appreciating the person's kindness, you have given that person an opportunity to practise generosity.

One Christmas Day I was in a Tibetan monastery in south India, doing a meditation retreat under the guidance of Geshe Wangchen, a Tibetan lama I knew. The fact it was Christmas flickered through my mind briefly, but I forgot all about it by the evening. I was just finishing my last meditation session of the day when Geshe Wangchen came in and asked me if everything was going well. Just as he was leaving, he gave me a pomegranate and wished me happy Christmas. This simple, unexpected gift, given with unequivocal generosity, is one of the most precious I have ever received.

On the cushion meditation:
GENEROSITY

Giving is an important practice, because it lessens attachment, especially to your ego. Yet people often give without a pure attitude. The following meditation will help you examine the motivations and intentions that lie behind different types of giving. It will give you insight into your innate grasping, both at things you desire and into the nature of yourself. Such insights help dispel the clouds of illusion surrounding who you think you are.

Begin the meditation session with 10–15 minutes of basic mindfulness meditation (see page 9), focusing on the breath.

- *Once your mind is calm, reflect on and analyse the following types of generosity described by the Buddha. There are many ways of categorizing generosity, but this one is a good place to begin. Buddha talked about three types of generosity: beggarly, friendly and princely.*

- *Beggarly generosity is when you give away things you don't want – perhaps items that are cluttering up your home or gifts you have been given that you don't care for. Consider how often you practise this type of generosity, or how often you are tempted to. Although better than giving nothing, such actions are not real generosity, and you should not feel you are being especially generous. You are not affecting your own* desires and needs in any way, so you are not challenging your attachment to any of the things you give in this manner. In fact, such beggarly giving can be just a way of tidying up your home. Reflect how often you practise beggarly giving, and examine if this makes you feel generous.

- *Friendly generosity* is when you freely share what you have with others. This involves giving away to others some portion of something you have and keeping some for yourself. This type of giving is an improvement on the beggarly kind. However, with friendly giving you need to check carefully your motivation and intention. For instance, you invite a friend to eat dinner with you, and you buy good food for the meal, but maybe the food includes things that you enjoy eating or are easy to prepare. Perhaps you expect your friend to bring a contribution to the meal and are disappointed if he or she doesn't.

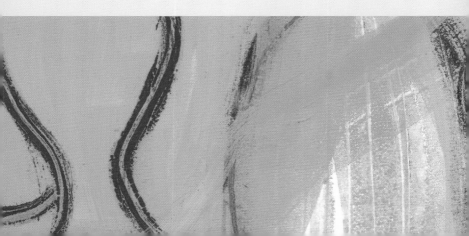

Maybe you expect an invitation, or gratitude, in return and are disappointed when this doesn't happen. Consider carefully whether you practise friendly giving purely, or whether you are pleasing yourself, or you have expectations of gratitude or return.

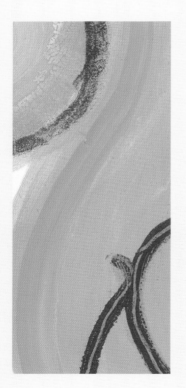

• Princely generosity is when you give away more than you keep, with no expectation of return. This is giving in order to give; the other forms of giving are giving in order to get. Princely giving is quite difficult to accomplish purely. See if you can remember an instance when you practised princely giving, and then carefully check your motivation. Was there any expectation of a return – even if it was only gratitude from the recipient? You should of course feel happy and good about yourself after princely giving, but check carefully whether the act has inflated your ego – 'I am such a generous and wonderful person.' Even trying to be 'good', or giving because you think you ought to, is a little tainted. Although giving in this spirit is not bad, nonetheless the aim in princely giving is to give purely out of compassion.

- *Bring your attention back to your breathing and allow your mind to calm for a few minutes, and rest in the insights you have gained from the meditation.*

- *Reflect that these kinds of giving are guides to help you give more authentically, with real generosity, and to help dispel illusions of generosity when in fact your motivation is not always pure. The meditation is not meant to make you feel bad because you don't always manage to give in the princely way. You can, however, learn some useful lessons about the subtle self-deception that exists in both beggarly and friendly giving.*

- *Generate the motivation to try to give in the princely way as much as possible in the future. Reflect that princely giving is done with compassion, and that you do feel happy, content and satisfied after giving in this manner. This peace of mind is priceless.*

PRACTISE GENEROSITY
on the go

Practising generosity does not always involve giving material gifts. Even the poorest person can be generous because the mind of generosity – the attitude underlying the act of giving – is more important than what, or how much, you give. The following activities can help you develop the true spirit of generosity and make giving part of your everyday life.

Give and receive

If you are stingy towards yourself, how can you be truly generous towards others? A Tibetan lama taught the following exercise frequently because he noticed that many of his Western students needed to learn how to be giving to themselves as a first step towards developing the mind of generosity.

Take a small everyday object, such as a stone. Hold it in your right hand. Notice what it feels like to have the stone. Feel appreciation for having and holding the stone. Now slowly transfer the stone from your right hand to your left hand. As you do so, feel that your right hand is giving the stone to your left hand. Remain conscious and aware of the sensation of giving. At the same time, your left hand is receiving the stone. Develop a feeling of appreciation that you are receiving something. Continue to transfer the stone back and forth between your hands for at least 10 minutes. Don't rush this exercise. Observe your feelings, noticing whether and how they change during the exercise.

The gift of life

In Buddhist countries it is traditional to buy caged birds, fish or other live animals from the market and release them. Since many of these animals are destined to be sold as food, releasing them saves them from certain death. Giving the gift of life is more precious than giving any kind or amount of material benefit. The following exercises are based on this principle of offering safety and refuge to living beings, including beings you don't normally care about.

The next time an insect lands on your arm, don't just thoughtlessly brush it away, which would probably kill it. Reflect that the insect is a living being, not so different from yourself in that it, too, has the right to live and in its own way to try to find happiness and avoid suffering. Blow the insect away gently so that you don't harm or kill it. In offering the insect safety, you are practising a powerful form of generosity.

After the rain, worms, snails and slugs seem to appear magically on footpaths, where they are prone to be stepped on and killed. Although you may not like these creatures, they still have the right to live. You could just avoid stepping on them, but they would remain in danger from other people walking there. A more effective gift of safety is to pick them up and place them to one side, away from the main walking area.

Consider whether you are willing and able to adopt a cat or dog from an animal rescue centre. If you are able to provide a long-term loving home to an abandoned pet, you will be practising the generosity of giving safe refuge to another being.

Small gifts to others

Try occasionally making some cookies, or buying some fruit, and taking these into the workplace to share with your colleagues. If this simple gift can be given without the expectation that someone else must do the same tomorrow, it can be a lovely way to be generous at small cost. Notice how the atmosphere changes as people chat and smile as they share the food.

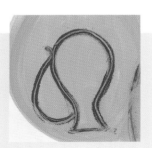

Even the poorest person can be generous ...

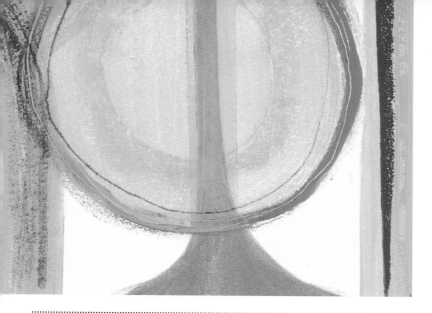

Charity on the street

The next time you see a beggar on the street and there are other people around so you feel safe, give a few coins to the beggar. Often you prefer not to see beggars and avert your eyes, but these people are in need, even if you feel they are lazy or not genuine. It is not easy to beg. Remember that the attitude of giving counts just as much as what is given, so don't just throw a few coins down in disgust. Make eye contact with the beggar, say something pleasant such as 'Have a nice day' and move on. Be careful not to enter into a conversation, as this might allow the situation to develop inappropriately – but giving what you can kindly is an act of real generosity.

WISHING LIFE AWAY

Patience is a sustained attitude of inner peace and tranquillity in the face of challenging and difficult circumstances. In Buddhism, patience is considered one of the six perfections, or ideal qualities, that help lead you towards a happy life and eventual enlightenment. Being patient means no longer reacting with anger when someone acts hurtfully or aggressively towards you. Instead, try to respond with love and compassion.

Suffering and dissatisfaction pervade life and are therefore inescapable. You can't prevent unsatisfactory circumstances arising, but you can learn how to deal with difficult situations skilfully. If you practise patience in the face of adversity, then you will both keep your peace of mind and behave in a way that doesn't cause further suffering. For example, if someone gets angry at you and shouts, you naturally tend to feel angry in response. What happens if you behave angrily too? The situation is aggravated because there are now two angry people. If instead you realize that you don't have to behave in the same way, and practise patience, the angry person will calm down much more quickly than they would if they were provoked any further.

Often when you find yourself in a difficult situation your reaction is to wish you were somewhere else, having an easy, pleasant time instead of suffering. This means first that you are not dealing skilfully with the difficult situation, and secondly that you are dwelling in a fantasy rather than in reality, and actually wishing this part of your life away. If you were to count up all the times you wished you were somewhere else, thereby avoiding engaging fully with the situation, you would realize that you have wished a lot of your life away. Patience involves being willing to accept, tolerate and deal with unpleasant and painful conditions as and when they happen, and being able to endure situations that you don't enjoy with consistent good humour.

Three kinds of patience

The Buddhist teachings offer a threefold classification of patience: the patience of forgiveness, the patience of accepting suffering and the patience of being able to behave virtuously.

The patience of forgiveness is being able to forgive immediately someone who hurts you, and not hold a grudge against them. The Buddhist teachings tell you that your enemy is your best friend. This sounds like a contradiction, but, if you reflect that your enemy is offering you opportunities to practise patience and thereby develop compassion and wisdom that will lead you towards enlightenment, it is easier to forgive your enemies and wish them well.

The patience of accepting suffering is of great practical use in your life, because suffering and dissatisfaction will inevitably arise. The Japanese Buddhist haiku poet Issa managed to transform suffering into joy by accepting it graciously. Issa lived the life of a poor, itinerant hermit, and his only daily companions were lice and fleas. He transformed his irritation at their frequent biting of him through cultivating patience to the point where he regarded them as dear

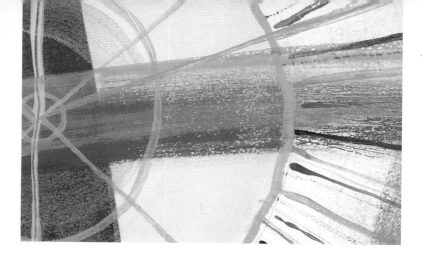

friends. Issa was preparing to go on a trip and wrote a haiku poem in which he addresses the fleas that lived on his body: 'Now, you fleas! You shall see Matsushima – Off we go!' His tone of companionable, compassionate friendliness towards the fleas is a powerful inspiration for us all to cultivate patience.

The patience of being able to behave virtuously starts with being patient with yourself and others as much as possible. Tolerance is an aspect of patience that helps you keep calm when you are faced with difficult circumstances and people. The spaciousness of tolerance, simply allowing things and people to be the way they are, helps prevent negative states of mind arising as a reaction to adversity, followed by unskilful acts. Staying calm and patient in this way helps to prevent bad behaviour caused by feeling angry and irritated, and helps you behave in a wise, compassionate manner.

On the cushion meditation:
PATIENCE

Impatience is the ego's response when things don't happen the way you would like them to. The ego wants things its own way, immediately, now. When your ego is thwarted, and it doesn't get what it wants, the response is frustrated anger. This creates a vicious circle: thwarted desire, impatience, anger.

The following meditation on patience examines this habitual pattern and offers insights into why it occurs. This understanding can help you break free from such negative behaviour.

Begin the meditation session with 10–15 minutes of basic mindfulness meditation (see page 9), focusing on the breath.

- *Reflect how often you don't get your own way, when your careful plans are wrecked by circumstances beyond your control, and things happen that you had neither foreseen nor wanted. How does this make you feel?*

- *Cast through your memories and recall an instance when your day went really badly. How did you deal with it? Analyse your responses. If you resisted what happened, clinging on to what you wanted to happen, then your dissatisfaction increased. You are powerless to stop things going wrong,*

and this is unavoidably unsatisfactory. However, if you simply accept the situation and deal with it patiently, you will suffer far less than if you fight against it. Ask yourself why you fight difficult circumstances when this only makes things worse.

- *Take the difficult situation you recalled above. Perhaps you didn't resist what happened and dealt with it calmly and wisely. If so, choose another situation when you did resist what was happening and struggled against it. Now, imagine how you could change this scenario by patient acceptance of circumstances. For example, imagine you are late getting to work because the train was delayed. This made you miss an important meeting and your boss was angry with you. He insisted that you stay late to make up the lost time, so you missed seeing your friend on her birthday. When you first knew that the train was delayed, instead of becoming agitated and feeling impatient, with your breathing shallow and your heart racing, imagine staying calm. This does not stop the train being late, you missing the meeting or your boss being angry, but at least you are not aggravating your own suffering. Imagine you sit calmly waiting, taking the opportunity to have a coffee and read the paper. There is nothing you can do about the late train, but by responding with patient acceptance you do not make yourself suffer further.*

- *Imagine you accept that you will miss the important meeting. Instead of railing against how unfair life is, imagine calmly reflecting on the best way to solve the problems and issues caused by missing the meeting. You work out patiently the best course of action. When your boss shouts at you, instead of feeling furious and choked up inside, you take deep breaths, stay calm, apologize (even though it is not your fault) and offer a positive solution to redress the situation.*

- *When your boss makes you work late, imagine phoning your friend as soon as possible and apologizing to her, and offering an alternative time to celebrate her birthday. Instead of ranting at her about your bad day, you try to console her disappointment and tell her you will make it up to her as best you can.*

- Reflect that none of your imagined patient responses changed anything in the circumstances. The late train, missed meeting, angry boss and disappointed friend were an unpleasant chain of circumstances which caused suffering. Yet by not resisting and fighting against these problems, but dealing with them one by one patiently and wisely, you did not increase your own suffering. Although you would feel a little upset by such a day's events, if you stayed calm and patient throughout you could go home and let the unfortunate day go, and get on with your life without holding resentment and anger. In this way, patience stops you increasing your own suffering, and helps you deal with misfortune as well as possible.

- Reflect upon and analyse this scenario from both angles: impatient non-acceptance and patient acceptance. Realize that increasing your own suffering through an impatient response to misfortune is foolish. Resolve to be as patient as possible next time you have a difficult day.

Staying calm and patient ... helps you behave in a wise, compassionate manner.

PRACTISE PATIENCE on the go

Putting patience into action can prevent you from making difficult situations worse. Remaining calm and patiently dealing with a challenging situation solves the problems more effectively and quickly than shouting angrily at someone. Practising patience is not easy, however. Remember that you will need to be patient with yourself if you try to be patient but forget in the heat of the moment. Here are some simple ways to develop patience in everyday situations.

Five deep breaths

Next time you feel angry, practise patience by taking five deep breaths before you say or do anything else. Let your mind dwell on the foolishness of an angry response as you inhale deeply five times, and exhale fully. Before you speak, check that you are not blaming someone, or being unpleasant, even if someone did something silly. Everyone makes mistakes, no one is perfect, and being patient and kind is the best response.

Stop rushing

We are so impatient that we tend to rush through life, trying to cram too much in, afraid we might miss something. The old saying of 'rushing towards the grave' rings

true more than ever in most people's modern, frantic, busy lives. Try
deliberately missing a habitual activity, such as going to the gym or
meeting friends for a drink. Instead, walk somewhere quietly by yourself
– in a natural setting, or at least in a park or by a river if you live in a
city – really slowly, and see how calm you feel at the end. Doing this
regularly will help you develop patience, and realize that it is fine to
miss activities sometimes, even if you enjoy them.

Choose the longest checkout queue

When you go shopping in the supermarket and reach the checkout, you
normally feel so keen to get out of the shop and get on with your life
that you choose the shortest queue. You can even see people dodging
from line to line, often getting it wrong and making their wait at the
checkout longer rather than shorter. What does all this effort achieve?
At best, you might save a few minutes, but in the worst-case scenario

you could find yourself waiting even longer and fuming in anger at the slowness of the other customers.

In this exercise, deliberately choose the longest checkout queue. Look at your reactions. It probably challenges your usual behaviour, and you might feel you are being stupid. Persevere, stand in the long line and watch your feelings. Once the shock of choosing a long line wears off, see how you feel. If you find yourself tapping your foot impatiently or repeatedly glancing at your watch, remind yourself of the purpose of the exercise – to develop patience.

Look at other people shuffling impatiently. What is the rush? What would you do with a few extra minutes not standing in the checkout queue? Since you are going to be standing there for a while, try to really be present in the situation. Be aware of your surroundings, think about how it really feels just to stand there; it is actually not that bad, not as awful as you thought it would be. When you stand impatiently in line, it is your own impatience rather than the queue that makes the situation unpleasant. As you relax into the experience of standing and moving forward gradually towards the front, remind yourself that you are developing patience, and reflect how helpful being patient will be when you encounter a really difficult situation.

Don't wish your life away

Accepting things for what they are, rather than wanting them to be something else, stops you wishing your life away. We all have a tendency to desire perfection, and when life's rich variety gives us experiences we don't like we try vainly to push them away. This light-hearted exercise helps you see the funny side of the unpleasant things in life, to realize they are temporary, accept them and let them go.

Imagine your life has been dealt to you as a hand of playing cards. As events unfold through the day, give each event a card number according to how you like or dislike it. For example, you drop your cup of coffee running to catch your train. Normally, this would irritate you and darken your mood. Thinking of this as a 'three of clubs' event can make you laugh at it and let it go. An attractive man or woman smiles at you – definitely a 'queen of hearts' moment! And so on.

Being patient means no longer reacting with anger ...

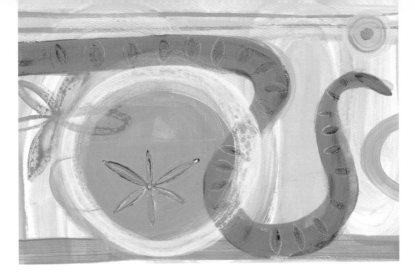

WHAT'S REAL AND WHAT'S NOT

We live in a world of flux, where nothing is fixed or certain. Views come and go, and what was once taken for granted is now disproved, such as the belief that the world is flat. This changing view of reality demonstrates the Buddhist principle that all views are 'empty of inherent existence' – that is, they are not intrinsically true but rather depend on who is looking, and when, and for what purpose.

Teachings on what's real are callled 'wisdom' in Buddhism. Wisdom has two levels of meaning. The conventional meaning is the way people usually think of wisdom – a quality of insight and deep understanding that leads towards logical and unbiased action. The deeper, or ultimate, meaning of wisdom is more specific, and can be defined as being wise enough to understand that everything you perceive – even yourself – is part of an interconnected web of causes, conditions and perceptions. In other words, things do not exist in the way you think they do.

Cultivating wisdom challenges your views of yourself and the world. You take your normal mode of perception for granted and believe in it absolutely, so it can be difficult to transform. However, consider the following. Water has a different reality depending on who or what is perceiving it: to a fish, it is home; to a drowning man, the enemy; to the thirsty man, delightful; to the physicist, a collection of molecules. Are there right and wrong perceptions here? Obviously not. Each perception of water is dependent on circumstances, causes, conditions and other factors.

When you transform your perception of the things and people of the world in this way, it is as if scales are falling from your eyes. You no longer mistake your perceptions and opinions about yourself and other people for 'absolute truth'. You no longer label your neighbour as 'an angry person'; rather, you see that frustrating conditions sometimes cause your neighbour to speak in an angry manner.

Recognizing that nothing exists independently and in its own right but is instead a result of causes, conditions and perceptions will

help you develop more respect for the whole web of life. For example, when you eat a slice of bread, reflect that it exists only because of the farmer who grew the wheat, the miller who ground the flour, the baker who made the bread and the van driver who delivered it to the shop. It also took sunshine, fertile soil and rain for the slice of bread to come into existence, so there are many interdependent factors involved.

This same kind of fresh perception can be applied to your view of yourself – the 'I' you take for granted. You usually regard yourself as an autonomous being, although just like the bread your existence depends on many different factors. How would you exist without parents, friends, housing, food and even the air you breathe? Once you let go of the fiction of an independent self, you will become aware of the vast intricate web of life as it manifests itself each moment.

This freedom from the narrow constraints of the self allows your actions to become spontaneously wise and compassionate. You will start to treat others as you would wish to be treated yourself, not from a sense of moral obligation but from an understanding that others and self are not different. So, next time you are involved in a dispute or an argument, remember that it is just two, or more, people holding different views, and that these views are ultimately empty of any definitive meaning.

Nothing to gain

Stay open, non-attached and non-grasping. Allow each experience to teach you something new by trying to see it with fresh eyes, beyond your usual perception. Once you let go of self-centred craving, life unfolds in the here and now. You will see the mystery of life and recognize the unique circumstances that make up each moment. Responding with compassion and wisdom to what you encounter rather than acting from self-interest seems the only way to be.

Someone once asked the Buddha what he had gained from enlightenment. He replied, 'I attained absolutely nothing from full and perfect enlightenment.' The Buddha's paradoxical answer reveals that enlightenment is not about attaining or *getting* anything. Rather, it is about *losing* your illusions and, in so doing, discovering that perceiving the world as 'absolutely nothing' is the greatest and most freeing attainment of all.

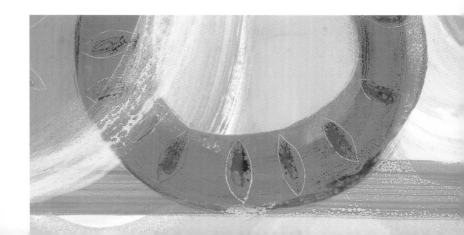

On the cushion meditation:
WHAT'S REAL

At the root of our deluded ways of seeing is the ignorance that conceives of objects and people, especially our own selves, as inherently existing. The force of this mistaken view gives rise to the afflictive emotions, such as anger, hatred, pride and jealousy. Meditating on the lack of inherent existence and the interdependent nature of all things will allow the inner life – usually obscured by clouds of thoughts – to flourish.

Begin the meditation session with 10–15 minutes of basic mindfulness meditation (see page 9), focusing on the breath.

• *Bring your attention to your sense of 'I'. Who is this 'I'? Who – or what – is it that is thinking, feeling and meditating? Can you locate the 'I' physically? Is it in your heart, or anywhere else in your body?*

• *After 10 minutes, bring the attention back to the breath, and allow the mind to calm. Don't fall into the trap of thinking you don't really exist. Reflect that there is an 'I' that exists; you get up every morning, go through your daily life and have many different experiences. It is how this 'I' really exists that is problematic.*

- *Start to inquire into the sense of 'I' again. You might perhaps think the 'I' is the mind, or is located in the mind. Yet the mind is full of ever-changing thoughts and sensations, arising and passing. How can this ceaseless, ever-changing flow be the concrete sense of 'I'?*

- *Reflect that you do exist, but are dependent on your mind and body, on causes, and on the unique set of circumstances that brought you to this present moment. When you hear your name spoken, it generates a strong sense of 'I', but consider that a name is just a name. It is only your imputation of self onto the name that generates the feeling of 'I'.*

- *Accept that you do exist – dependent on your mind, body, causes and conditions – but that your sense of 'I' lacks any inherent existence. The absence of 'I' is the emptiness of the self. Finish the meditation with this thought: your sense of 'I' depends on the ever-changing flow of mind and body, but there is no solid, independently existing 'I'.*

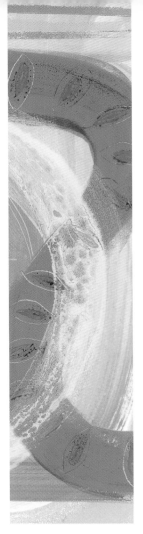

EXAMINE WHAT'S REAL on the go

A man needed wood from his garden shed at dusk. As he opened the
door and peered through the gloom, he jumped back in horror, thinking,
'Help! There's a snake!' He still needed the wood to light his evening
fire, though, so he peered closely at the inside of the shed to see if he
could see the snake moving. Slowly he became bolder as he saw the
snake remain motionless, and he crept forward. Suddenly the moon
came out from behind a cloud, and he saw in a flash that what he
thought was a snake was in fact a hosepipe.

This story shows how you absolutely believe what you see,
together with feeling a whole range of emotions, but your perception
can be proved wrong in a moment. The man in the story probably felt
relieved, but also foolish at his mistake. For a brief time, he would stay
open to the fact that his perception of other things might also be

wrong, but then his strong sense of 'I' would reassert itself. Using the story as an inspiration to let go of your certainty of the truth of your perceptions, try the following exercises to loosen the certainty that your perceptions and views are absolutely correct.

....

Let go of your own viewpoint

Grasping at your own particular way of seeing can cause conflict with other people because you forget that there are other valid ways of seeing. When you are next in conversation – or heading towards an argument – with someone who sees things differently from you, pause. Are you judging the person according to their view? Has your opinion become so rigid that you now think it is the only worthwhile opinion and will fight to defend it? Instead, try to let go of your viewpoint – it is, after all, only a view, dependent on your vision of the world, not an absolute fact. Instead, be open and listen to the other person's point of view. You might learn something that helps you understand the emptiness of views.

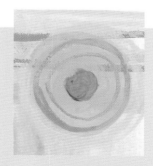

Cultivating wisdom challenges your views of yourself and the world.

Watch your dreams

Do you remember waking up from a nightmare and feeling scared because it seemed so real? Dreams can be so vivid that their impact can carry over into waking consciousness. Yet a dream has no reality at all, although the archetypal images in dreams carry messages from the unconscious to the conscious. Try recollecting your dreams every morning, even if you have only a few moments before you must get up. Notice how real they seemed, but recollect that during the dream there was no sense of normal life. When you wake up, even if you remember them vividly, your dreams bear no relation to waking reality.

Different scenarios

Insurance accident reports often show that each witness saw a completely different scenario. To each person, their version of events is real, and everyone else's must be wrong. You can try this out with a friend or two. Take a window seat at a café and watch the street outside. Sooner or later some event will occur: someone bumps into someone else, someone drops their bag, someone runs into the road and a car has to brake. Each time something happens, get each person in your group to describe exactly

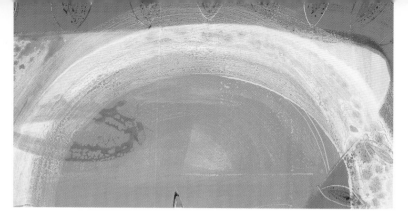

what they saw. You will probably end up with as many different versions as there are people. Don't be drawn into a discussion, or even an argument, about what actually happened; simply observe that your own version of events is not necessarily 'correct', or the only valid version. This will help you to be less attached to your own viewpoints.

Dissect a cup

Pick up a cup and look at it. What makes it a cup? If you break off the handle, is it still a cup? If you plant a flower bulb in the cup, is it still a cup or has it become a flowerpot? How does the cup exist? When you hold it, the cup seems to exist in its own right, to have inherent existence. However, when you consider that once the cup was a lump of clay that a potter shaped and then fired, you can see that the cup lacks inherent existence. Without the causes and conditions surrounding the cup, it could not exist. As you ask questions about how the cup exists, you will start to realize that things do not exist inherently.

JOYFUL EFFORT

We need determination and resolve to keep on meditating and following the Buddha's path. It is not easy to meditate every day; it takes great energy to transcend procrastination and laziness. Nor is it easy to practise compassion and wisdom; it takes many years of dedicated practice for these virtues to arise spontaneously in the mind. So, in the same way that we require firm determination to start meditating, we need joyful effort to keep going.

Changing your old habitual patterns and instincts and learning new, positive and skilful ways of being through meditation is an ongoing process. So you need to keep checking how you are doing in a realistic, non-judgemental and unsentimental way, and not just rely on your initial wish to practise meditation. For example, you can easily fool yourself that you are meditating properly when in fact you are simply sitting there lost in thoughts and daydreams. However, there is little point in giving up when the going gets tough, problems arise or you discover you are not really trying in your meditation, as these are moments of great opportunity to learn and grow. This is when joyful effort and enthusiastic perseverance become your best friends.

Joyful effort can of course be applied to all aspects of your life, helping you to do efficiently the worldly things you want and achieve your ambitions. However, the Buddhist teachings inform us clearly that the best application of joyful effort is to help with our spiritual practice. You need first to consider your attitude towards your meditation. If your attitude is only to follow a set of instructions blindly and rigidly, then your meditation may be only making you miserable, and there is not much benefit in meditating in this way. If, however, you remind yourself frequently and thoroughly of the great benefit to yourself and others from practising meditation, this will help you cultivate joyful effort.

The great Tibetan Buddhist meditator Milarepa practised meditation in the most austere conditions. He lived in a cave high in the mountains with few possessions and very little to eat. In fact, in pictures he is often painted green, since nettles were one of the few things he had to eat. However, Milarepa was so happy with this way of life and so full of joyful effort in his meditation practice that he became famous for composing and singing songs about how wonderful it was to have the opportunity to meditate like this. These joyful songs are still sung and recited by Tibetan Buddhist teachers today as an inspiration for their students.

Three aspects

In the Buddhist teachings, there are three aspects of joyful effort that you can apply to meditation and following the Buddha's path.

The first aspect is understanding the great value in practising an authentic spiritual path, and developing confidence that you can do it. If you approach meditation feeling helpless and inadequate, wanting meditation magically to solve all your problems, then your attitude is

too passive. You think that meditation will take care of you, and that you don't have to do anything more than sit on a cushion for a while. In this case you develop joyful effort by reminding yourself often of the great virtues and benefits of meditation, compassion and wisdom. This gives you strength and courage to carry on.

The second aspect is maintaining joyful effort despite all the setbacks and problems you encounter. Meditation is a continual, ongoing practice to train the mind to be calm, spacious and clear, and is not confined to sitting once a day or a few times a week. So you must have great resolve not to give up. You can make the firm decision not to lose energy and enthusiasm, and maintain joyful effort by meditating on the many benefits of meditation and following the Buddha's path. For example, perhaps you have been meditating daily for a month but you feel despair that your mind is as full of racing thoughts as when you started. By reflecting that a calm mind is definitely worth striving for, you will meditate again with renewed joyful effort.

You carry on developing and maintaining your meditation practice over a period of time, but you still need some extra impetus once in a while. This is the third aspect of joyful effort, the encouragement to follow your meditation practice through, day after day. For example, this means not giving up watching your breath after five minutes one day when you are feeling particularly lazy. Remind yourself that you have innate Buddha nature, and that one day you will be enlightened, to give you an extra impetus to keep on meditating with joyful effort.

On the cushion meditation:
USE JOYFUL EFFORT

It takes a surprising amount of mental energy to meditate, and applying this energy skilfully is using joyful effort in meditation. This energy needs to be applied skilfully for the meditation to be effective in training the mind and transforming ingrained negative habits. Energy is neutral; it is neither good nor bad in itself. It is how you use energy in meditation that is important. So you need to apply joyful effort carefully in your meditation practice to try to remain calm and attentive throughout every session.

Begin the meditation session with 10–15 minutes of basic mindfulness meditation (see page 9), focusing on the breath. During this time, reflect that the liberation from suffering that Buddha discovered is worth the effort of meditating as well as you can, as often as possible. Consider that this continual striving is in itself joyful, because it leads to the greatest and most genuine happiness – enlightenment.

- *Resolve to use joyful effort to best effect in your meditation, and carry on watching the breath. Now assess how you are in the meditation. Are you feeling a little dull or sleepy, or is your mind full of racing thoughts or disturbing feelings? Carefully note how your mind is at this moment, paying attention to every little detail and nuance.*

- *If your mind is full of racing thoughts, perhaps you need to bring a little less energy and effort to your meditation. Think of your mind as a fine musical instrument that needs delicate and frequent tuning to work at its best. If your mind is strung too tightly, it will race, with thoughts rushing through. Relax into the meditation, and watch the breath without trying too hard. Let thoughts go as soon as they arise, but without suppressing them. Be gently attentive to what is happening in your mind, but do not get drawn into the individual thoughts.*

- *On the other hand, if your mind is currently strung too loosely, you may be feeling a little dull, lethargic or sleepy. Although your mind may feel calm and peaceful, you need to investigate closely that the mind is still attentive and aware. It is easy to slip into a dull state of mind, but think that your mind is simply calm and therefore your meditation is going*

well. Analyse this calm state carefully, and assess whether your mind is genuinely calm but fully alert and aware, or if perhaps your mind is sleepy and lethargic. It is possible to fall asleep while meditating, but this is not the desired outcome.

- *If you feel your mind has become a little dull, you need to bring more joyful effort and energy into the meditation. Think about tightening the strings to bring a taut, energized quality to your mind. Pierce the dull heaviness of your mind with fresh inspiration and resolve to be fully attentive again. Don't force yourself too hard, or otherwise you may overstimulate and excite the mind. Gently sharpen your attention and direct this to the breath. Aim to be fully aware with clarity and calm.*

- *Using joyful effort in this way is refining the meditation process, which will help you make the most of your meditation. By constantly checking whether your mind has slipped into dull lethargy or overexcited racing you can fine-tune the mind into an alert, clear, calm state. This*

Following the Buddha's path and meditating is deeply rewarding.

technique will take time and energy – and joyful effort – over many meditation sessions to develop and become really dynamic, but it will eventually make your meditation more effective.

• *It is easy, once you have been meditating for a while, to slip into bad habits, such as indulging your thoughts and daydreams, or just sitting there in a sleepy lethargy. Bringing joyful effort into the meditation practice helps to counteract this complacency and keep the process fresh and sharp. You can think of joyful effort as a light but steady intention, energized with inspiration that will help your awareness remain steadfast throughout your meditation sessions.*

PRACTISE JOYFUL EFFORT
on the go

The practice of joyful effort in everyday
life means not giving up wise and
compassionate behaviour when you feel
selfish, angry or lazy. Remind yourself that
your kind and skilful actions towards
others are not only beneficial for them but
also contribute to your own happiness and
eventual enlightenment. Consider that this
is what you want to experience and so it is
worth striving for, and that the practice of
joyful effort in everyday situations can
help you realize this goal.

Milarepa's joyful effort

You can see from Milarepa's story on page 116 that joyful effort is not
authentic if it is used only to gain material wealth or worldly benefit,
but applying joyful effort in your meditation practice can generate a
wonderful, spontaneous happiness. True joyful effort is when you strive
to be free from worldly attachments, because you know they don't lead
to happiness. In the following exercises, you can use joyful effort in
daily-life activities to transform your negative mind states and feelings,
and to be of benefit to others.

Wash the dishes

Washing the dishes after a meal is many people's least favourite daily task. It can even cause arguments when someone tries to wriggle out of their turn. Acknowledge to yourself that there is nothing you can do to change the fact that the dishes need washing and, if it is your turn, that this is simply the case. You can change your attitude towards washing the dishes, however, by applying joyful effort, and this can make a real difference to the task. Joyful effort can make any household chore an engaging way of practising spiritual wisdom.

Instead of feeling negative and resentful about washing the dishes, and wishing you were sitting down relaxing, generate joyful effort. Remind yourself that by doing the dishes yourself someone else does not have to do them. Feel happy that you can offer another person the opportunity to relax. Don't just rush through the task to get it over with as quickly as possible, because this makes the task into a chore. Take your time, embrace the task fully and find some aspect you enjoy. For example, try looking at the light reflections in the soap bubbles, how pretty and

ephemeral they are. Take pleasure in the sparkling clean dishes as you stack them to dry. Consider how the task is not so bad if you practise joyful effort while washing the dishes.

Don't put off till tomorrow what you can do today

Laziness – as differentiated from rest and relaxation – can develop into a bad habit, and prevent you doing the things you want to. Joyful effort is the greatest antidote to laziness in all of life's activities and motivates you to get on with what you need to do, as stated in the traditional saying above. Select a task that needs doing now, but that you have put off doing because you don't want to do it. This could be cleaning your

room, writing an essay or report, weeding the garden or any other job
you dislike doing. Generate joyful effort, and reflect that by engaging
fully with the task now you will transform your usual procrastination.
Apply yourself wholeheartedly to doing the job, from start to finish.
Once the task is completed, rejoice in its completion and appreciate the
finished result.

....

A final thought

Just before Buddha died, one of the last things he said was,
'Impermanent are all created things. Strive on with awareness.' Buddha
was referring to the importance of joyful effort, together with
awareness, to awaken to your true nature and attain enlightenment.
Whenever you are feeling tired or depressed, remember Buddha's words,
and strive on with awareness.

*Resolve to use joyful
effort to best effect in
your meditation...*

INDEX

ACKNOWLEDGEMENTS

Executive Editor Brenda Rosen

Managing Editor Clare Churly

Executive Art Editor Sally Bond

Designer Darren Bland and Pia Ingham for Cobalt id

Illustrator Anne Wilson

Production Controller Aileen O'Reilly